On Becoming
The Art of Seeking

&

Some Gas
A Collection

Written by:
Adrian Berumen

Cadmus Publishing
www.cadmuspublishing.com

TABLE OF CONTENTS

On
Becoming

For you who refuse
To stop your
GREATNESS from
Being exposed

…Keep at it
Your time will come
Because this
Shall pass

FOREWORD

"WE CANNOT BECOME WHAT WE NEED TO BE BY REMAINING WHAT WE ARE."
-MAX DEPREE

Who needs another inmate trying to tell them what to do? I've asked myself that many times. My goal is to encourage you to do. Intentional becoming, now-a-days, seems to be one of the toughest things to do. Some may believe it's nearly impossible, and I'd almost agree with you if you said, "Because I'm in jail." I hope that you will be open to me because the same way I've accomplished putting this material to print while I'm incarcerated, you have the "DO" to reach this kind of GREATNESS plus some! Take heed, fellow mate, motivation awaits.

ONE:
THE STRUGGLE
IS REAL

*"THE MAN WHO MOVES A MOUNTAIN BEGINS BY
CARRYING VERY SMALL STONES."*
-W. FAULKNER

Can you remember how you felt after calling more than once, and you still couldn't get someone to answer? Those feelings of frustration, anger, and on-my-own aloneness fill your body and mind. It can truly be devastating. I've seen that small situation be very influential to a person's decision making. They'd become so willing to make life-altering choices from unanswered calls. The worst part about this is most of us don't ever think in terms that our choices (especially the small ones) can change our lives.

What about being in the dorm, cell, or on the yard, and hearing that one dude brag about how good his visit was? Better yet, you hear how he was going to be ordering a whole lot of soups and honeybuns from the commissary this week, because his visit looked out with some cash. Weeks, months, maybe years, go by, and you still never receive any sort of similar treatment. You begin to envy those few who continue to thug, yet are so favored. Some of us are easily influenced and follow the footsteps of the hoodish activity to earn a bit of respect, love, and, hopefully, a spoon of spread while others have a hateful mindset, wasting all thoughts and attention trying to find reasons to justify their belief on the hated individual.

I've met guys who've become hard-hearted toward their families because of missed calls, no visits, and lack of support. We act like they owe us their time and money they worked for. We demand that they answer the phone at any and all times. We feel they should make us a priority at least once a week by booking a visit, not considering any sort of cost for gas or parking. We have no regards toward their emotional or physical accounts whatsoever.

If you're not in denial, you will agree that this is how most of us start out when we first come to jail (some still think like this years into a prison sentence). This being said if you have any support to begin with.

I know it can get lonely and tough. Trust me, I know. When you're facing hefty charges; stacked on that you have to dodge the mental shots fired at you by those miserable inmates you bunk or cell with, almost every day. I know how it can be when you have to shower and poop amongst other men. I remember the first week of being incarcerated in the county jail. I didn't want to go make a sit down because I was embarrassed. I remember another man telling me I had to shower, "Or else…" Those were intimidating times.

I know, deep down, they didn't intend any harm. That's just the language spoken in jail – violence. And really, who wants to be around a smelly eighteen-year-old kid? The sad part was, I didn't like being a dirtbag. I was merely embarrassed at being naked amongst other men.

Jail is tough, and sadly, many of us earned our residence here. (To those who have fallen victim to this system, I'm sorry it's such a ruthless experience. I hope it shapes you for the better!) My goal is to shine a light in this cave. Many of us are molded, while some crack and others completely break.

I highly dislike pondering on what this time in jail is not doing for me. Why should we waste seconds on how this system is corrupt, or how jails and prisons should be done away with?

Truthfully speaking, I believe this system works if we can understand how to make it work. I'm talking about shifting our thinking. Believe me, there's a whole lot to "become" from this situation that is rough, limited, and lonely. I can see great potential in this jail time. There's some shifting we must do though. There must be some transformation in our thinking before we can see a difference.

"I AM THE SOURCE OF MY OWN IGNORANCE."
-BRUCE LEE

TWO:
THE PRINCIPLE
SHIFT

"LIFE IS NOT SIMPLY HOLDING A GOOD HAND.
LIFE IS PLAYING A POOR HAND WELL."
-DANISH SAYING

PRINCIPLE: A GENERAL OR FUNDAMENTAL LAW, DOCTRINE, OR ASSUMPTION; A RULE OR CODE OF CONDUCT; A PRIMARY SOURCE:
-THE MERRIAM WEBSTER DICTIONARY

I sat bear-butt next to a man once; I was glancing at a picture so beautifully taken, you could find it on the cover and throughout the pages in a National Geographic magazine. Believe it or not, I sat amongst three other men. Squatting shoulder to shoulder with no separating walls or any sort of privacy.

As we laid waste amongst each other, the need for a magazine was absolutely necessary for distraction from this unnatural and revealing poopage scenery. Yet, this particular time it became different. The man beside me noticed the great Taj Mahal portrait I stared, daydreaming at.

He went on striking a conversation about how the Taj Mahal would be a nice trip to take someday. We chatted awkwardly. Of course, the other men joined in. At that moment, it clicked. Being exposed to this small comradery, despite our actual (toilet) circumstance, we managed to create good feelings. This toilet situation didn't have to be awkward. This was the perfect example of how powerful we really are. One point to highlight is the willingness we portrayed: to converse while on the toilet. I must emphasize that this information I am sharing can only work if you are *willing*. Only if you accept.

Before I get into the principle this book intends to inspire you to meditate on, I'd like to mention that I am incarcerated in the Los Angeles County Jail, still awaiting trial, for over seven years. Los Angeles is said to have one of the toughest county jails to pass through, due to inner ruthless mentalities that fill the cells, dormitories and law enforcement positions. So, do away with any thought that fills your mind, saying, "It's easier said than done," or "You don't know how tough it really is." Be open-minded to this principle that has brought me countless opportunities.

So back to this principle; This understanding you must not

forsake! It's the saying I'm sure we've all heard many times – IT'S IN YOUR STATE OF MIND! The way you think creates a perception of your situation. That becomes the foundation to all your beliefs and choices. Since this saying is the principle in my life, then it drives my thinking further, and I create the belief that *the process is perfect.*

The process of life is not lacking. It is meant to operate in perfection. I've empowered myself by valuing this current time, despite me facing a criminal charge that holds the possibility of sending me to prison for twenty-five years to life. Stop for a moment and grasp this law I'm placing in front of you.

You think it's hard to simply change your state of mind when you're focused on the courts giving you the maximum sentence, or when your lawyers are acting like they are really trying to help you? It is! No doubt about that. I'm not telling you to pretend like you're not under huge amounts of stress. I'm telling you to slow down and try a different pair of glasses on. You should question why you're thinking that you're never going to go home. Ask yourself, "Can I change the way I feel?" You may not know the outcome, but you can certainly contribute to the income.

A friend of mine once spoke about how we think our way into these situations. I like the part when he said we should be able to think our way out by changing that thinking. He's been incarcerated for twenty years, and served twelve of those years on Saint Quentin's Death Row. His verdict was reversed three years ago. He is the proof – when you change your thinking, you can change the results.

I challenge you to believe this process is perfect. I'll give you some points to support this belief and watch as this principle "in your state of mind" affects your might - empowering your actions. Opportunity to fulfill your desire is then inevitable.

"THE ONLY DIFFERENCE BETWEEN STUMBLING BLOCKS AND STEPPING STONES IS HOW WE USE THEM."
-AMERICAN PROVERB

THREE: PARTING THE PRINCIPLE

"THE UNEXAMINED LIFE IS NOT WORTH LIVING."
-SOCRATES

Your clock is ticking.

"GUARD WELL YOUR SPARE MOMENTS. THEY ARE LIKE UNCUT DIAMONDS. DISCARD THEM AND THEIR VALUE WILL NEVER BE KNOWN. IMPROVE THEM AND THEY WILL BECOME THE BRIGHTEST GEMS IN A USEFUL LIFE."

-RALPH WALDO EMERSON

The first point I'd like to stress may have already stressed you out. It is the Exacto knife to this masterpiece. *TIME!* Time, in itself, can set you ahead, or set you far behind. Too many men fail to realize that this *time* in jail is a result of our state of mind. So, on it goes being wasted. Why? Because we're in jail, defeated. Hopeless. Pessimistic about the whole situation.

I won't lie. It took me about two years before I actually started making my time count. Yeah, I wasted about two years, and believe this, I still find myself wasting time (on worry) by dwelling on things completely out of my control. It's tough, but it's not impossible. This is a daily battle that every human being must show up for. Continue to bear with me while I lay more foundation.

Does a diamond shine bright a soon as it's dug up? You see, a diamond is molded by the grand jeweler. Diamonds are said to have specific, one-of-a-kind, cuts and edges. That's what gives a diamond its value. That's what causes a person to spend a quarter of a year's hard-earned money, and sometimes even more, to merely place it on the finger, or a pair of ears, of a loved one. You may notice some people go into debt because of a diamond's value. The value developed from the *time* used cutting and edging this raw gem.

Are you getting the picture? If you can believe this process is perfect, then you can see this time stuck in a cell or dorm of value. As you perceive how important this time is, your mind will start to focus on "cutting and edging."

Again, it's hard, but not impossible! Most of us never view these moments through an open mindset. We instantly assume hopelessness and powerlessness. Limitations do that. We feel weak and low. The isolation from family, friends, and nature can cause this. Mentally, we become less of a person because we feel or believe that we are stuck. That's exactly what the locked doors are supposed to do. That can be a contribution to slowing this time down. I've seen men decay; eventually, they try and "check out." I'm talking about suicide. Don't let this negative idea motivate your attitude to this type of action. You can apply this energy elsewhere. That brings me to our next point. *Focus!*

"PEOPLE ARE NOT DISTURBED BY THINGS, BUT BY VIEWS WHICH THEY TAKE OF THEM."
-EPICTETUS, ANCIENT GREEK PHILOSOPHER

Don't just hear me, listen!
"SINCE YOU CAN'T CHANGE TIME, YOU MUST
INSTEAD CHANGE YOUR APPROACH TO IT."
-J. MAXWELL

"It was too late." Keyword: "Was." If you're merely attentive to what you didn't do or what you could have done, who and how you let someone down, it will eventually be too late.

[If you made it this far into the book, I believe you're following with this process being perfect. A perfect opportunity. We have the power of passing it up and wasting it or tending to it. Continue to follow and don't quit now. Quitting is for your bad habits.]

Many of us were lacking the powerful trait of focus. We focused on all the wrong things. This is the reason almost one-hundred percent of us came to a place like this, and because we lack the value of focus, we have difficulties eyeing this time incarcerated as an advantage.

Consider this, we don't have to pay bills. We get fed and clothed. We have access to showers, and a bonus: The different personalities and cultures we deal with daily will only improve our communication skills. Why wouldn't we consider this as an opportunity to get ahead? You'd rather be free with none of these benefits? I'd probably make that choice too, but that's not an option, so move on from that idea!

Now remember, we all focus, but those of us who have started to focus on the *art of focus* have one difference: Our cutting and edging process is distinct. We focus on *priorities!*

Many of us outside of these locked doors had no clue what was important (or maybe we were selfish). We focused on a lot of trash. A lot of things that pulled us back and devalued us. A lot of things that disappointed our loved ones (some of us still do!).

That is why we now find ourselves stuck on thoughts of who and how we let people down. We find ourselves in places like these; feeling or thinking that it's too late. Hopeless and stressed out.

This isn't something to worry about though. Being incarcerated can be a beneficial place to become focused on priorities.* You may receive tons of backlash, but that's the reason to become disciplined. Prove people wrong. Show them who you've become from what you once were. *It's in your state of mind.* If that's the new principle you stand by, then it only makes sense to stand firm despite any criticism, backlash, and negativity toward your new self.

Take a moment now, and focus on what is a *priority*. Ask yourself, what does it mean to be important, and add it to your vocabulary!

IMPORTANT: SIGNIFICANT

SIGNIFICANT: HAVING MEANING; HAVING OR LIKELY TO HAVE CONSIDERABLE INFLUENCE OR EFFECT.

This all may be hard if you still believe the negative thoughts of being powerless and stuck, or if you continue to ponder on your bad feelings. The goal is to change your mind! This leads me to the last point I must tell you about – *attitude!*

"YOU CAN'T REACH THE TOP UNLESS YOU START CLIMBING."

-ALAN KILPATRICK

The Might
"YOU ONLY LIVE ONCE. BUT IF YOU WORK IT RIGHT, ONCE IS ENOUGH."
-FRED ALLEN

Quote me on this: Your attitude is a contributing factor to your priorities. I know my biggest problem in focusing on what should have been a priority was due to the fact that I gave my power over to people and to situations. It was my reason why I acted. My choices became reactions, and I blamed others for making choices in my life. My attitude was the result of my surroundings.

The weather can be a hell-of-a-thing, but the rain still wouldn't stop many from going out. I believe a persistent person invented the umbrella. That person didn't allow the weather to affect the power of choice. Persistence must be a characteristic of an emotionally intelligent person. It's the characteristic of a person who chooses the desired attitude!

As inmates, it can be difficult to see our power to choose. I had to learn from trial and error. I don't remember any schooling or elderly guidance on choice (or maybe I wasn't listening until I finally came to jail). If you're not getting taught this before you come to jail, your chances of learning it become slim. The only reason I say this is because we all inherit the false belief of having no say whatsoever, due to us being in jail.

What's that common saying we all hear throughout our sentences? "Bro, this is jail." I won't lie, I've said it a few times (OK, maybe a lot more). Then you have the inner jail politics trying to control the population. On top of that, you have the courts pressing you. All of these negative feelings and stupid beliefs immediately become a part of our general thought process. Simply stated, our beliefs influence our attitudes, and attitudes influence our choices.

If you can't empower yourself, then your attitude will be the direct result of the way you allow yourself to feel. Or, as you may believe, as others make you feel. But, yeah, that's incorrect, and you know this now. Why? Because you have the power to feel otherwise.

So, how do you become intelligent emotionally? It certainly starts in your thinking. Since the beginning of this book, if you are being influenced, you've already started learning how to be intelligent emotionally.

"A MAN IS ABOUT AS BIG AS THE THINGS THAT MAKE HIM ANGRY."
-WINSTON CHURCHILL.

*A quick power tip on emotional intelligence: We have many things in life we have no influence or control over. But we also have things we do have some sort of influence or full control over.

The number one thing we all have control over is how we react to something, or to someone, that stimulates us. Stimuli causes feelings. Unusual stimuli may cause us to feel a negative way, only because most of our feelings come from habits which are direct results of hostile beliefs (created over years of physical or mental abuse). These can be conquered.

Some persistence with this new understanding we have in development will eventually create a new habit – the powerful habit to choose how you want to feel and act towards various points in life. Anything outside of your influence is unnecessary stress. That's none of your business. Leave that to whomever can have an impact.

If you find yourself dealing with people or places that you know you have no control over, remind yourself to keep your feelings in check. If you wish to express any emotion, show some sympathy (this is another tip for being effective – in relationships).

*Your attitude is key to staying focused. Attitude is the secret to enabling you to focus in on what's significant and what is not. That all becomes the result of what you can control and what you can't control. This is the beauty of having the mindset "it's in your state of mind" despite our circumstances.

By believing "this process is perfect," I have flourished into the GREATNESS I was meant to be. The wonderful thing is, we were all created to stand and perform in GREATNESS. Too bad many of us are unaware of this might we have access to, which hinders us from taking responsibility. Our responsibility is denied. We continue to claim that we are victims of society. It truly is glum.

This last point – attitude – is what creates possibilities. It's what opens that door to opportunity.

"IN ORDER TO DO MORE, I'VE GOT TO BE MORE."
-JIM ROHN

FOUR:
THE EFFECT

"THE SECRET OF WALKING ON WATER IS KNOWING
WHERE THE STONES ARE."
-HERB COHEN

<u>Time</u> – The Exacto Knife to this masterpiece; the advantage.

<u>Focus</u> – On what's important; priorities.

<u>Attitude</u> – Your energy toward possibilities; emotional power; choice.

These three points should be formed together to support our new perception – *the process is perfect*. This is growth.

Have you ever witnessed those instant moments a flower blooms, the ones we never seem to catch in action? Probably not. They are too sly. This is exactly what occurs as you intertwine these points (what did the wisest man, King Solomon, say? "Two are better than one, and a threefold is hard to break"). What springs up? Accountability. You become responsible.

<u>Accountable</u>: **Answerable, responsible.**

<u>Responsible</u>: **Liable to be called upon to answer for one's acts or decisions; able to fulfill one's obligations; reliable, trustworthy; able to choose for oneself between right or wrong.**

-The Merriam Webster Dictionary

I hope a lightbulb turned on in your head. This is great news. The pressure you feel and must go through is the molding of your GREATNESS. It is the prickly thorned stem on a beautiful, blushed, red rose. It's potential waiting to be unveiled. The beautiful thing about potential is, you don't have to be out of jail to fulfill it. You can pursue it right now.

There's not a day that goes by where I find no struggle. You have to welcome it instead of running from it. Give thought to that beautiful, spikey, rose once more. When you happen to prick yourself on the stem, does that stop you from plucking it for that special person you most adore? No! This jail time shouldn't neither. These circumstances should not determine our success. We can own our life and stop blaming another for our choices.

Yeah, OK, I know, maybe your choices haven't been the greatest and are humiliating. But own them. The shame shall pass. You claiming ownership creates the opportunities to change them. The pressure can get intense, but I can guarantee, the pressure will prime and smoothen the surface of this canvas we call life. (If you know nothing of painting, priming is necessary.) A smooth canvas is the best platform to produce a more stunning piece. The struggle is merely the beginning of your luminosity. It's what makes this process perfect.

"ACTION MAY NOT ALWAYS BRING HAPPINESS,
BUT HAPPINESS IS IMPOSSIBLE WITHOUT ACTION."
-BENJAMIN DISRAELI

FIVE:
LET ME SELL IT
TO YOU

*"THE ONLY THRILL WORTHWHILE IS THE ONE
THAT COMES FROM MAKING SOMETHING OUT OF
YOURSELF."*
-WILLIAM FEATNER

Effort

I've discovered if someone left it up to me, then it's up to me! That's an opportunity. You shouldn't wait to act with effort. Your responsibility goes from being the candle to being the fire. It would no longer be waiting, but willing. No doubt, this is an opportunity for your value to rise.

I'm sure you've seen those men who are always happy. It's rare, but they're all over jail and prison. These men have taken control of their lives to some point. I am almost completely confident, because jail is a negative experience, and for them to experience this happiness and joy, it is only due to them choosing to overcome this miserable realm. They've made the choice to be responsible.

Why not empower yourself to make your life better? Why not make your time in jail worthwhile? I observe this as the greatest opportunity of believing *it's in my state of mind*. It's an energy source. One that will last as long as you're alive and are able to THINK. As long as we tap into this thinking, it will start to show in our character, impacting anyone watching. This will generate a whole other rush. This is what makes the effort worth it.

Spotting

"WHEN ONE IS TRULY READY FOR A THING, IT PUTS IN ITS APPEARANCE."

-NAPOLEON HILL

Let me give you another reason to change your thinking. When you open your mind and shift your thinking, you obtain the benefit of discovering other opportunities. The key to eyeing opportunities is not in being ready for it, but in being willing for it. We miss so many opportunities because we can't eye it. Our eyes are focused on the time being horrible. Our attitude is unwilling to go through thick and thin. To be ready for an opportunity can short arm you. Why? Because you're ready for something specific. It's like being picky with opportunity. Bad news: There may be tons of different types of opportunities, and you're missing them. This can have a reverse effect on your attitude.

Oops! You gotta shift your thinking. If you can believe *it's in your state of mind*, you can reason with the process being perfect, transforming your attitude to a willing one. You'd start focusing in on a plentiful of opportune jail time. Shift your thinking. Allow yourself to bloom. Become more.

"SOMETIMES WHEN I CONSIDER WHAT TREMENDOUS CONSEQUENCES COME FROM LITTLE THINGS ... I AM TEMPTED TO THINK ... THERE ARE NO LITTLE THINGS."
-BRUCE BARTON

SIX:
OH, AND
SOMETHING
ELSE.

"APPRECIATE YOUR OPPORTUNITIES AS YOUR
GREATEST ASSETS AND THEY WILL CONTINUALLY
INCREASE IN VALUE."
-A. BEE

A tip

Tug-of-War can be a struggle, but a fun one. Especially when one side fails to hold any more resistance. They go plunging dead smack into a puddle of mud, one on top of another. It can give off a great ear-to-ear smile. I like to believe that game idea was a creation exemplifying life.

As we seize the unlimited opportunities our new pair of glasses are allowing us to discover, be ready to experience resistance. Some good advice: Never cease to keep in thought, loud and constant: **hard work is encouragement to work hard!** This hard work is an opportunity, so take advantage of it and work hard. Grit it out! My boy Craigen likes to label his "gritting it out" as maximization – leaving what is, better than it is. He knows it's an opportunity, so he's not merely playing not to lose. He's playing to win! Craigen gives one-hundred percent on top of his one-hundred percent.

The tip: Right beside shifting your perspective, if you will allow yourself to make maximization a habit, you can't go wrong.

Example: Craigen and I have been given the chance to work with mentally ill inmates. When we arrived, directions to assist group therapists with their classes, along with helping those mentally ill with cleaning, had been given to us. We followed orders.

If you never had any relations with someone battling severe mental illness, it can be tough to communicate with them. We had no prior training in regards to mental illness or care taking, and honestly, the years incarcerated before working with these patients had taught us to shun these "crazy people." Usually the shunning turned into violence, which is the complete opposite of what this job intends us to do. If you put that flawed, closed, mindset with those inmates in dire need of help, imagine what that would look like. Not so clever.

It's now been more than three years, and we've published a book all about the mental health position we created here in the jail. The book contains a training curriculum for anyone who wishes to implement the role of a M.H.A., a six-week course developed for mentally ill patients and has brief information on the main, severe, mental illnesses. This took a lot of trial and error, a lot of research on mental illness and how to be effective in communicating, as well as a lot of resilience, but we accomplished it. We weren't instructed to, but we did. Not only did we work hard at this hard work, we maximized this because we had seen this as an opportunity. The doors of opportunity continue to open. That's what comes from maximization.

"WHATSOEVER A MAN SOWETH, THAT SHALL HE ALSO REAP."
GALATIANS 6:7

SEVEN:
BRING BACK TO
MIND

"ONE OF THE MOST COMMON CAUSES OF FAILURE
IS THE HABIT OF QUITTING WHEN ONE IS
OVERTAKEN BY TEMPORARY DEFEAT."
-NAPOLEON HILL

A daily dose

It's no mystery that this process is a rude one. At times, you may find yourself physically in the hole, as called in prison: the S.H.U. (solitary confinement), or for some it can be a mental captivity. But count this only as temporary defeat. I like to say death is the only end of this energy I'm sharing with you, so if you're still alive, it's not done, keep stirring!

This is the trait that will set you apart. This is what I call overtime. Overtime sets apart the greater from the great. Persist and persevere! I heard this song say, "When we fall down, we get back up." Adopt that thinking. Rewards are released when you refuse to give up.

Being mighty will always be a battle. You will win some and you will lose some. This should create zeal, not discouragement. *Remember, you can choose. This knowledge has empowered you. You'll need to remind yourself daily. Reexamine. Reconsider. Recap. Review. Wherever these options are necessary, remind yourself. You can think and make choices. I know this sounds so basic as common sense, but too many of us don't do this (this chapter is absolutely necessary!).

*Reminder – There is a difference in my attitude and the attitudes surrounding me. The difference: I have control of mine and no control over any other than mine. That's an understanding supporting my powerful beliefs. I must recall this before I go onto the battlefield each day. This reminder will change things...

"THE GAP BETWEEN YOUR VISION AND YOUR PRESENT REALITY CAN ONLY BE FILLED THROUGH COMMITMENT TO MAXIMIZE YOUR POTENTIAL."
-J. MAXWELL

EIGHT:
A BONUS

*"WHAT LIES BEHIND US AND WHAT LIES BEFORE
US ARE TINY MATTERS COMPARED TO WHAT LIES
WITHIN US."*
-OLIVER W. HOLMES

On purpose

You were formed on purpose. What specific purpose, I can't say. That's something you will have to discover. I can say the general purpose of life is potential. To reach your greatest potential.

Our first few months in jail (for some it may be years), we go through some depression, because, in our mind, our purpose was taken from us. As I said earlier, we feel powerless, limited, lonely and humiliated. So, of course, the result is depression; as if we have no purpose. We do! If you remember *it's in your state of mind,* you bring the general purpose back. You empower yourself to choose. Your choice is there to take you to the greatest heights you can possibly go.

Of course, some critical thinking must go along, but do you get the point? This whole process is perfect. When you can begin perceiving this, your life will change. Results will change. Circumstances will change. Not the difference in itself, but you being able to make a difference is the general purpose of your life. Once again, you can choose to do that.

Grab a hold of this truth, and your circumstances will never be able to define you. You'd be amazed when you see things around you change for the better. You will become effective in your life, and you'll impact the lives around you. A result of walking on purpose.

"WE SHOULDN'T LOSE SIGHT OF THE FACT THAT WE HAVE IMPACT WE MAY NEVER SEE."
-BETTY ROGERS

NINE:
LAST BUT NOT
LEAST

"JUST DO IT."
-NIKE

Get active

I challenge you to be powerful! Review this material over and over until it becomes habitual. As my elder, S.R. Covey, states, **"There's no effect without discipline."** I'm not kidding about the unlimited opportunity that awaits you. When you start to focus on what you can control, you will find this time as a blessing, instead of a curse.

I often hear guys speak on how they weren't arrested, they were rescued. Well, OK, so what now? One of my mentors, Mr. Maxwell, says it like this: **"Though you can't go back and make a brand-new start now, you can *start now* and make a brand-new end."**

Johann Wolfgang Von Goethe said, **"Things that matter most must never be at the mercy of things that matter least."** This *time* now matters most; you will never get this time back. What you can't control, like your circumstances you find yourself in (this jail time), matters least. Deal out how you're going to act in regards to what's important, and reap the benefits plentiful. Why be the sad story when you can be a great one? You're so worth it, you just gotta believe it!

"THE DIFFERENCE BETWEEN GREATNESS AND MEDIOCRITY IS OFTEN HOW AN INDIVIDUAL VIEWS A MISTAKE."
-NELSON BOSWELL

Afterword

Pardon my flaws. Only insist on taking what can be used and maximize it! *Remember: This is an opportunity. My strategy to simplify and shorten common information seems to be an easier, beneficial approach. Now what will you do with it? Incorporate this information and dare yourself to be more, or debunk me. Either way, you'll be seeking a greater you, because both of those directions require a heavy dose of "On Becoming…"

The Art
Of Seeking

For you who persist
through life's
hardships.

May the rest
of the world
find love in seeking the
wonders of
everyday!

INTRODUCTION

"THE MOMENT ONE DEFINITELY COMMITS ONESELF THEN PROVIDENCE MOVES TOO. ALL SORTS OF THINGS OCCUR TO HELP ONE THAT WOULD NEVER OTHERWISE HAVE OCCURRED. A WHOLE STREAM OF EVENTS ISSUE FROM THE DECISION, RAISING IN ONE'S FAVOR ALL MANNER OF UNFORESEEN INCIDENTS AND MEETINGS AND MATERIAL ASSISTANCE WHICH NO MAN COULD HAVE DREAMED WOULD COME HIS WAY."
-WILLIAM H. MURRAY

To start, this is not me claiming to be an expert. This is me sharing my observation and giving inspiration on how I reach success despite my circumstances. Success is possible while we are limited. The problem with reaching success is it's an art, while not many people are artists.

In this new generation, everything is made to be fast and easy; when it comes to seeking, people lose motivation. For us behind the locked door, with no access to the fast and easy, we have no other choice. You strive, or you don't. My goal is to encourage you to be as great as you're meant to be. Although it may be harder than average, if you can find motivation, you will stand out from the usual and secret forces will be unleashed, both to support and oppose you. A reward in itself.

Many people choose not to seek, because they don't want to feel resistance. They miss out on rewards and still have to feel the struggle. This is what living is – resistance and sprints. Why not embrace the process and reap some reward while you're at it? Don't be as those who fail to exist during their existence simply because they believe there won't be hardships if they avoid them.

I understand these crucial circumstances can be discouraging.

For some of us, it blows our candle flame completely out. No drive to seek remains in you. Success is still possible.

The understanding of this art is why few move up and too many fall behind. The art of seeking lacks the label "Important." Seeking becomes rare. Many of us choose to settle for less. It makes no sense! When I see greater things, I don't understand why we would ever settle for anything other than more. I'm not talking about becoming greedy. I'm speaking on what we are created to walk in – GREATNESS! I believe that we can get that which we want, we just have to really want it. We may fail many times, but that may be what it takes. Some of us may as well achieve at a first go, yet we never know if we never begin. Don't allow your situation to be your excuse. I know too many people who excuse themselves by stating, "I'm in jail." Consider this: Publishing this book is a great accomplishment. Although it didn't come easy, it sits in front of you as a finished product. Many wonder how it was accomplished despite the lack of access. That, my friend, is known as the ART of seeking.

"FOCUS ON CHOICE, NOT CONDITIONS (YOU CONTROL YOUR COMMITMENT)."
-TONY ROBINS

ONE:
SEEKING

"THE SECRET OF OUR SUCCESS IS FOUND IN OUR DAILY AGENDA."
-TAG SHORT

Seeking is not as tough as we believe. There's definitely a struggle to it, but like I've said before, to struggle is a part of life. Why then don't we seek? First off, its importance is not expressed as it should be.

Most of today's seeking is done out of habit, or out of desire to instantly receive what one wants. For some, the struggle is enough to lose passion. It becomes an excuse. For others who naturally seek as a habit, or for the sake of desire, it may take them to great heights, but they never pay close attention to this process as a vital piece of the art. Don't get me wrong, there are many who know what it takes to see success, and I'm sure they would agree with this book.

For us who find ourselves in jail, we instantly take on the label of being restricted, limited, and bound, setting us up to stay inside the box. That's our excuse not to do more. That becomes our right to settle for less. I'm almost sure this is the reason you're reading this. Let's change that.

"HE WHO CANNOT CHANGE THE VERY FABRIC OF HIS THOUGHT WILL NEVER BE ABLE TO CHANGE REALITY; AND WILL NEVER, THEREFORE, MAKE ANY PROGRESS."
-ANWAR SADAT

I'm sure you're familiar with the game "Hide and Seek." I'd like to compare the art of seeking to this game. The seeker searches for those who hide. One searches and searches and searches, until one finds. That's it. Until you find! Seems very simple. A tough process, but never impossible. In jail, it can seem more intense, but in time, achievable. Good thing we're in jail where there is plenty of time.

I think we can conclude that seeking is simple, but there is certainly more to the mechanics of it. If we go back to the thought of Hide and Seek, there is a clear goal and direction for the one who's chosen to be "It." The It person is seeking those who hide.

What is it that we are seeking? We must first have a direction.

"TWO MEN LOOKED FROM PRISON; ONE SAW MUD,
THE OTHER, STARS."
-DALE CARNEGIE

TWO:
DIRECTION

"NEVER LESS CAN NEVER BE LESS."
-KOBE BRYANT

If you have no direction, where are you going? With no direction, you're wandering. Wanderers waste time. They go on through life letting time leave them behind. For us stuck in jail, we can't allow time to go on without us giving it meaning and value. These are moments we will never get back. Time can either leave you forgotten or set you ahead. You choose!

Your direction should always be thought about first when you're seeking. There is no such thing as seeking if you don't have that which is "hiding." Begin by asking yourself, "What is it that I desire? What am I looking for? What!"

The "What" is what you're looking for before you start moving to success. Is it material? Is it people? Relationships? Help? Comfort? The beautiful thing is, you can seek anything; a way out of jail, if that's your true desire. If there is a will, then there is a way. I would suggest, as you think on which way you'll be headed, grab some paper and a pencil and write your thoughts. An idea will continue to be an idea until you make the first step and write it down.

When I first thought about publishing a book, that's all it was for a long time. I thought about it with no action at all. I'd go on and forget about it. That's what happens if it remains only as a thought. You'll forget about your direction. You'll never begin seeking the success of your idea. (I would bet that you allowed tons of million-dollar ideas pass on by.)

One day, I started writing poetry to express my feelings and the idea of publishing a book sprang up once more. I wrote it down and added details. It made me dig deeper. I started asking myself: *Why?* Why do I want to publish a book? The why gave me more direction. I got specific. It became real. It may have been a simple idea on paper, but it sure was tangible. This is what you call a step closer to success. I felt motivated. I became hungry to see the idea come to pass.

Why is very important to establishing an attitude that will exceed difficulties. What and Why are how you discover the worth of what you're seeking. Without value, there is no motivation to succeed.

In search for the why, I also ask a very important question: Do I wish to make an impact in my world, or make an impact in the world? (This is a question on core value. Your what and why should line up with the answer to this question.)

There is no wrong answer. This is important to answer, because you will discover if this direction you've developed is truly important to you. Your core values are what you stand for. They are what you're willing to struggle for. You'll resist anything otherwise. If your direction lines up with your core values, you know it's important to you and your attitude will be unwavering. Your willingness will overcome and make any kind of resistance seem petty.

RISK TO WORTH

I once watched this movie called *Heat*. The star actors were Robert DeNiro and Al Pacino. Are you familiar with it? At one point in the movie, Robert DeNiro mentions the "Risk to Worth" method. Him and his crew were the bad guys of the movie (they could be good depending on the way you looked at it). They were heist men. I wouldn't quite say they were wise, but the "Risk to Worth" thinking seemed to be clever. Every heist they involved themselves with, they would place it on the scale – **risk to worth**. If it was far more worth the risk, they would do the job. If not, they passed it up.

In life, before we begin seeking, it would be smart to consider Robert DeNiro's thinking. His method compliments your core value (you're only ever willing to take risk for that which, deep down in your core, you value). We must be wise and weigh it out so we don't go and waste a bunch of life seeking only to give up on our quest, because we suddenly believe it's no longer worth seeking. This is how you will create the willingness. This is why you will set your direction as a priority. This will be the push to your direction.

"HE IS FREE WHO KNOWS HOW TO KEEP IN HIS OWN HANDS THE POWER TO DECIDE."
-SALVADOR DE MARADIAGA

THREE:
FOR YOUR
CONSIDERATION

"IF YOU GO OVER THE EDGE, YOU FALL."
-STEPHEN R. COVEY

As for some extra wisdom, you should definitely think about potential pitfalls! Pitfalls are important to consider when you are developing your willingness. Go ahead and ask yourself: "What can be a cause of struggle as I put 'might' into seeking?" I like to say that we shouldn't prepare for certainty, we should prepare for grit. You don't necessarily need to be prepared for how to deal with pitfalls, but it would be smart to consider possible hardships so that you're not suddenly knocked over or out by an unexpected blow. This is also important, because it verifies if you're willing to seek out your direction until you accomplish it.

"100% OF POWER LIES BETWEEN WHAT HAPPENS TO US AND WHAT IT TURNS OUT TO BE."
-A. BEE

FOUR:
GET ACTIVE!

"THE MOST IMPORTANT WORK YOU WILL EVER DO IS ALWAYS AHEAD OF YOU."
-STEPHEN COVEY

So far, we've discussed the idea and attitude of seeking. I'd say the only thing missing now is action!

"THAT WHICH WE PERSIST IN DOING BECOMES EASIER – NOT THAT THE NATURE OF THE TASK HAS CHANGED, BUT OUR ABILITY TO DO HAS INCREASED."
-EMERSON

I can sum it all up in one word: Persistence! It's easier said than done, but keep in mind that the done begins in the said. We're merely making our first steps. Let's look at seeking for what it really is. Many can say, "If you want to see success, all it takes is persistence." But what does persistence really mean? Why isn't persisting as easy as it sounds? Persistence requires the combination: **GRIT** – Tenacity, fortitude, and resilience.

When I started seeking out how to publish a book, I met many difficulties. I'm talking about years of difficulties. It took fortitude, what I like to label as the **endurance** of persistence.

Fortitude: Strength of mind that enables one to meet danger or bear pain or adversity with courage; courage in the face of difficulties.

The publishing difficulties were distinct from the actual writing difficulties. Let me tell you why; if you're looking to make sales, you will need an audience, a buyer and a demand for your idea.

I'm talking about, if you're sincere about being a writer, and wish to pursue it as a career (and find success), then you have to either relate the message or tell the story so your audience receives it. It requires much time and extensive thinking to create your book outline, because, of course, you will need to strategize. So, an outline is essential. You will have to edit and, most likely, rewrite multiple times. (I hope I'm not discouraging you!)

Take a moment to remember how jail – the lack of resources – contributes to the hardships. We don't have access to computers. You know that's a struggle in itself. Nothing but paper and pencils. I'm talking about sharpening pencils (the short golf pencils) over and over; writing and erasing so that you preserve paper, or else you won't have enough. This requires **tenacity**. I like to say this is the *power* of persistence.

Tenacity: Not easily pulled apart; cohesive, tough.

It all sounds basic, yet it requires a lot of **willingness**.

We arrive at this last piece of grit. I've went through the whole process of writing, editing, and hustling, so that I can purchase stamps and envelopes for packaging, only to be turned down, let down, and some of my work robbed (this one person helped me put it all together, and posted it up on Amazon, only to suddenly disappear. He claimed to be a Christian leader). Yet, here I am, a motivated seeker. Persisting! This is where **resilience** becomes important.

Resilience: An ability to recover from, or adjust, easily to change or misfortune.

Although I had done so much to succeed, much of my work didn't display my grit, the persisting. I'm sure some of my work went on to be successful without me, and it raised hurtful feelings because of all the grit and trust I invested. Hard-heartedness and insecurity haunted me for some time, yet resilience made me golden. Along with fortitude and tenacity, resilience was the final piece to becoming effective in persisting. You will experience setback, there's no doubt about that! The question is: **Will you incorporate grit? Will you persist?**

"WE ARE NOT UNCONSCIOUS BEINGS TO BE MERELY PULLED OR PUSHED AROUND."
-UNKNOWN

Here are some tips and quick highlights of keys to persistence.

A: Don't stop.

"WE MUST NOT CEASE FROM EXPLORATION AND THE END OF ALL OUR EXPLORING WILL BE THE PLACE FOR THE FIRST TIME."
-T.S. ELLIOT

When you're headed in a direction, you must keep in mind that it may seem as if it's taking forever to reach success and you constantly find yourself failing over and over, causing a stall in reaching your milestones, but this does not mean it's impossible to achieve. That is where you must implement fortitude. It will require discipline; trying over and over will evolve into discipline, so continue in persistence and it will turn into a habit (this is what you want). Consider: Some suffering may be important to forming a discipline! If it was easy, wouldn't the world be filled with disciplined people? Learn to get comfortable with being uncomfortable.

"GREAT PRESSURE BEGETS GREAT RESULTS."
-A. BEE

B: "I feel..."

"HAPPINESS DEPENDS ON HOW I ARRANGE MY MIND."
-NORMAN VINCENT PEAL

Prepare to feel all sorts of feelings. Happiness, grief, anger, irritation. But perceive those feelings as if someone is poking you to remind you that you're alive and you must remain determined.

Go on and enjoy the way you feel, and use it as energy. Or, if the emotion isn't so pleasant, affirm yourself. Tell yourself, "I don't have to feel this way I'm feeling." This is where you must incorporate tenacity. Own those emotions and don't let them own you! When you're seeking, you're claiming the power to choose and act. You've empowered yourself. Believe that and show it in your actions.

"YOU'RE MORE LIKELY TO ACT YOURSELF INTO FEELING THAN YOU FEEL YOURSELF INTO ACTION."
-JEROME BRUNER

C: Some help.

"EVERYTHING NEGATIVE... IS AN OPPORTUNITY TO RISE.:
-KOBE BRYANT

Who says failure can't be the help? Failure should be checked off as a lesson learned! Adopt this way of thinking, and you're well on your way. It is tough, so get tough. A little struggle will define you, and the more you find yourself struggling, you can claim you're one of those great people in the making. Let it be some motivation. Let that be a reminder to stay prepared, not for certainty, but for grit. Be a person of resilience, embracing life's setbacks, ready for the bounce back.

"THE GEM CANNOT BE POLISHED WITHOUT FRICTION, NOR MAN PERFECTED WITHOUT TRIALS."
-LUCIUS ANNAEUM SENECA

<u>D: The beauty of it.</u>

"WHEN A PERSON SHOWS YOU WHO THEY ARE,
BELIEVE THEM."
-M. ANGELOU

Persistence is the key factor of seeking and the process that defines you. It will show you who you are, or who you're capable of becoming. It's a struggle that creates beauty.

A rose begins as a small seed. The process consists of digging up soil, burying the seed, fertilizing, watering, and patiently waiting (as the growth of the rose requires many suns). As time passes, coinciding with a persistent gardener, the rose begins to grow and, eventually, blooms. It turns out to be a beautiful gift for the one you believe is most deserving.

As a flourishing rose requires a persistent gardener, to publish a book requires a persistent writer. The achiever will require a persistent seeker. Without persistence, there will be no success. But I promise the reward is worth far more than every moment the persistent person struggles.

"NO ONE CAN DO GREAT THINGS WHO IS NOT
THOROUGHLY SINCERE IN DEALING WITH
ONESELF."
-JAMES RUSSEL LOWELL

FIVE:
THE REWARD

"CHAMPIONS DON'T BECOME CHAMPIONS IN THE RING. THEY ARE MERELY RECOGNIZED THERE."
-J. MAXWELL

You better believe this whole process of seeking is a reward in itself. The suffering along with repeated action is the development of discipline. When you find yourself successful after this process, you will never settle for less. You will know how it feels to accomplish and receive more and will now desire more. That's the life of a disciplined person.

Of course, this is the underlying reward besides achieving your ultimate goal you sought in the first place. You will achieve it if it's truly your desire. Anything is possible. The question is: **Do you believe anything is possible?**

"SELF-DECEPTION CAN COST THEM THEIR VISION."
-BILL EASUM

SIX:
SIX OBVIOUS
ENEMIES TO A
WILLING SPIRIT

If you've made it this far in the book, it's clear that you're truly in a pursuit of greatness. You desire becoming an artist of seeking. But just because you're reading about it doesn't mean you will seek soon after. There will be some enemies who will oppose your dreams, goals, and directions; mainly a battle within self. Some will be complacent and others will be defeated by these foes. Let's consider them...

Laziness

LAZY: DISLIKING ACTIVITY OR EXERTION; ENCOURAGING IDLENESS; SLUGGISH; DROOPY, LAX; NOT RIGOROUS OR STRICT.

We all would agree that the lazy person would rather do nothing than something. Laziness has the power to destroy relationships, and lives if *you allow it to.*

Don't confuse exhaustion or tiredness with being lazy. They key here is to recognize when one needs to rest and when one needs to turn the TV off, make the bed up, and strive.

"SHOW ME WHAT YOU CAN DO; DON'T TELL ME WHAT YOU CAN DO."
-JOHN WOODEN

Ignorance

IGNORANT: LACKING KNOWLEDGE; RESULTING OR SHOWING LACK OF KNOWLEDGE OR INTELLIGENCE; UNAWARE, UNINFORMED.

Ignorance installs a puffed-up ego. I run into many men in here who I would nominate their photo to be placed in the dictionary next to the definition of ignorance. I'm sure you can relate. I remember when I knew it all. Or at least I thought I did (I think we all go through this phase). The key is in recognizing our ignorance. I was only fooling myself from a lot of opportunity. Ignorance will bring you to a brick wall sooner or later, and crush your motivation, ending your drive to seek any further. Watch out, and remember, when you really come to know, that's because you've discovered you know not.

"TO BE CONSCIOUS THAT YOU ARE IGNORANT OF THAT FACT IS A GREAT STEP TO KNOWLEDGE."
-BENJAMIN DISRAELI

Selfishness

SELFISHNESS: CONCERNED WITH ONE'S OWN WELFARE EXCESSIVELY OR WITHOUT REGARD FOR OTHERS.

I'm sure you're familiar with, "You get what you give." There is more opposition to selfish ways than there is help. Seeking is already tough as it is, for you to be selfish will pile on more difficulties. It can become discouraging to the striving spirit.

This will be a good time to reevaluate your core values and maybe make some changes.

"WE HAVE MADE AT LEAST A START IN DISCOVERING THE MEANING IN HUMAN LIFE WHEN WE PLANT SHADE TREES UNDER WHICH WE KNOW FULL WELL WE WILL NEVER SIT."
-ELTON TRUEBLOOD

Lack of Structure

"ONE REASON GOD CREATED TIME WAS SO THAT THERE WOULD BE A PLACE TO BURY THE FAILURES OF THE PAST."
-JAMES LONG

Most of us who lack structure see no value in our time. We are in jail, limited, but that shouldn't have to affect what we do with this time. If we can't envision the value in this time, setting priorities and organizing our actions are useless to us. Don't fall into regret later, for never taking advantage of now. Find the momentum, motivate yourself and begin moving. Think of a plan and write it out. Get ahold of yourself, physically and emotionally. Enable yourself. **NOW** is an opportunity to pursue greatness, and it will surely affect your time later.

"WHATSOEVER A MAN SOWETH, THAT SHALL HE ALSO REAP."
-JESUS OF NAZARETH

Insecurities
INSECURE: UNCERTAIN

"YOU CAN'T LEAD A CAVALRY CHARGE IF YOU THINK YOU LOOK FUNNY ON A HORSE."
-JOHN PEERS

Another way I'd like to define insecurity is: To be wavering
WAVER: TO FLUCTUATE IN OPINION, ALLEGIANCE OR DIRECTION.
The willing spirit must be confident. No hesitation. The insecure person fears otherwise. The one who fears may never make a choice, and to choose is most important in the art of seeking. The remedy is to find some support in every choice you make. Ask yourself, "What will allow me to be confident?" Then go do that!

"...FOR HE WHO DOUBTS IS LIKE A WAVE OF THE SEA, DRIVEN AND TOSSED BY THE WIND. FOR LET NOT THAT MAN SUPPOSE THAT HE WILL RECEIVE ANYTHING FROM THE LORD; HE IS A DOUBLE

MINDED MAN, UNSTABLE IN ALL HIS WAYS."
-THE EPISTLE OF JAMES

Procrastination

PROCRASTINATE: TO PUT OFF, USUALLY HABITUALLY, DOING SOMETHING THAT SHOULD BE DONE.

Procrastination sets you behind, and then it leaves you behind. It's easy to put things off until another time. The hard part is getting it done later. Why wait for later when you can do it now? Do it! Just go do it! Even when you don't want to. Make that a habit. Lacking structure can go hand in hand with being a procrastinator. If we misunderstand how valuable time is and how organizing our actions play a big role in reaching success, we will continue to procrastinate through life. We will settle for less. We will be making a huge mistake. Don't you claim a less destined value. Don't let a character mistake hold your willing spirit back. Seize your desire and you'll unleash more of it. Don't procrastinate on it.

"THE PROBLEM PEOPLE HAVE IS THAT THEY WANT THINGS TO STAY THE SAME, YET ALSO GET BETTER."
-J.C. MAXWELL

There may be many enemies to you who strive, but as I said, these are the obvious. These are the few I continue to deal with today as I seek. If only we consider them will we not be fooled into being satisfied with less.

"IT IS NOT THE CRITIC WHO COUNTS, NOT THE MAN WHO POINTS OUT HOW THE DOER OF DEEDS COULD HAVE DONE THEM BETTER. THE CREDIT BELONGS TO THE MAN WHO IS ACTUALLY IN THE

ARENA; WHOSE FACE IS MARRED BY DUST AND SWEAT AND BLOOD; WHO STRIVES VALIANTLY; WHO ERRS AND COMES SHORT AGAIN AND AGAIN; WHO KNOWS THE GREAT ENTHUSIASMS, THE GREAT DEVOTIONS AND SPEND HIMSELF IN A WORTHY CAUSE; WHO, AT BEST, KNOWS IN THE END THE TRIUMPH OF HIGH ACHIEVEMENT; AND WHO, AT WORST, IF HE FAILS, AT LEAST FAILS WHILE DARING GREATLY, SO THAT HIS PLACE SHALL NEVER BE WITH THOSE COLD AND TIMID SOULS WHO KNOW NEITHER VICTORY NOR DEFEAT."
-THEODORE ROOSEVELT

SEVEN: A BONUS

*"THE BEST REASON TO CARRY A HANDKERCHIEF IS
TO LEND IT."
-FROM THE INTERN*

Before I end this, I challenge you to incorporate the law of service into your daily routine – lend a hand instead of looking for one to use. If you can value giving a helping hand repeatedly, this will have an impact on your character. It will turn into a habit of selflessness, eventually creating discipline. Powerful and beneficial to your attitude and grit when it comes to your seeking. The world may just be ready to give back.

*"YOU'RE NEVER WRONG TO DO THE RIGHT
THING."
-MARK TWAIN*

Let this be your opportunity to claim your greatness. Success awaits the hand that is willing, and that which is hidden will soon be found by the artist of seeking.

*"WE ARE DEVELOPED THE SAME WAY GOLD IS
MINED. SEVERAL TONS OF DIRT MUST BE MOVED
TO GET AN OUNCE OF GOLD. BUT YOU DON'T
GO IN THE MINE LOOKING FOR DIRT, YOU GO IN
LOOKING FOR THE GOLD."
-DALE CARNEGIE*

AFTERWORD

It's not a secret! I would merely say this topic isn't emphasized enough. An artist of seeking walks in purpose, on purpose. This truth should inspire the rest of us who have settled to rise up, take what life has to offer, and pursue what life holds in the hidden safe. Let us live through these days in GREATNESS. Why must we barely survive? Let us overcome our days and walk as people who welcome life's rigid moments for the sake of desire and capability.

Some Gas

To you who
At times
May fail
To refuel.

You are
GREAT STUFF
Waiting
To be
Unveiled.

FOREWORD

If we can change the way we think, we can change circumstances. The seven plus years I've been in L.A. County Jail (and still reside as I write), a good word has done nothing but transform my life for the better. I hope these next 31 days my words do the same for you.

Day One

"Circumstances should NEVER determine your success."

This book is evidence that circumstances *do NOT* make us. I am in jail. I've been in jail for seven years. A county jail, with no idea of the sentence I have to serve, which makes things harder. Yet, *I chose* to thrive. I decide if success is possible now!
You can too...

DAY TWO

"Things get tough because we were created to overcome."

Scientists have proven that the mind, body, and spirit will adapt to stress. Extreme stress – they've proven we can overcome. I am convinced that this is part of our purpose.

DAY THREE

"The man who walked on the moon began by
crawling on earth."

The truth is: to start is the toughest. It's easier to dream and
come up with ideas. The challenge is in the first steps. Don't wait,
just do it. You will regret never making a move more than any
mistaken choices.

Day Four

"Failure has *potential*."

Without failing, the process won't be complete. Therefore, great achievement comes from failure, and as long as you *will* to do more after failure, then it **will** come to be more.

DAY FIVE

"The pressure you feel is just the *molding* of your greatness."

Diamonds won't be a beauty without the pressure that molds their gleaming edges. We, as diamonds, must be defined. As we come to understand this, may we welcome life's hardships as opportunities to become our greater selves.

DAY SIX

"Make the critics an asset.*"*

Pick up a book. If it was published by an official company, they must have seen potential and moved the book to have sold thousands, maybe millions, of copies. Bringing in ten times the amount of copies they sold in cash. That, my friend, is a genius of a product made by the critics of the company. If the book had not gone through countless drafts, criticism, and approval of editors, it would not have been published.

Day Seven

"There is beauty in life's ugliness."

As thorns prick the tips of your fingers, pulsating pain brings much more meaning and beauty to even the reddest of fluffy roses. Only a person of shifting perspective can unveil this wonder. Will you then consider this point of view merely to bring more color to your life? What is there to lose?

DAY EIGHT

"Weaknesses now are only for now."

Convince them that you should be judged on your progress. Therefore, build off what's broken. And if they stone you, build a castle. Remember the old saying: "What doesn't kill you, makes you stronger." You *should* get stronger – that's up to you. And, if it kills you, it won't matter. You'll be dead.

Day Nine

"It begins in a state of mind."

The key to seeing success is **staying inspired**. The good news: the frame of your thinking is in your hands. Your inspiration, motivation and ideas for creation all begin in your little (big) head! Your perception then is the authority of your response.

DAY TEN

"Don't wait until it's too late to be great."

I once heard a saying: "Life is like a coin. You can spend it on whatever you want, but you only get to spend it once." You'd regret less from your mistakes than from never making any at all.

Day Eleven

"Knock until someone answers."

Keep buzzing like the flies that buzz around your face until it gets a reaction from you. Keep your actions persistent until they produce. Don't waver. Remain resilient. Hold onto hope. Then the mountains will move! You'll see if you resist from quitting.

Day Twelve

"Though there may be opposition, the choice to defeat or be defeated is yours."

John Creasey received 743 rejection slips from publishers before a piece of his work ever got published. Eventually, he published 560 books, which have sold more than sixty-million copies. You define your destiny, but only if you wish.

DAY THIRTEEN

"Last place finished the race."

This, my friends, is another step to greater heights. Does not the one who grits to the end possess the character that inevitably brings about grand achievements? Don't you dare say you're done until it's done.

Day Fourteen

"Those truly strong remain strong. Be strong!"

Requiring zero fibers of strength, it is easy to give up. While many speak of their might, very few show it. Make sure your actions speak louder than your words, and please, don't doubt your heart. It's more than capable of surprising you.

Day Fifteen

"Stay prepared for the rainy days, so that even on those days you'll shine bright, as if the sun was out."

Preparation is the opportunity to take *the lead*. While everyone was altered by weather, one person decided to invent the umbrella. That person decided to deem that "falling rain" an opportunity to persist harder toward success.

DAY SIXTEEN

"Thoughts can be impossible to the one whose head they're not in."

If we allowed the outer beliefs to affect our final decisions, we would be as the many unknown accomplishments that now lay in graves all over the world. Did you know that Albert Einstein, Edgar Allen Poe, and John Shelley were all expelled from school for being mentally slow? If only they would have believed that nonsense, our world would have taken big losses!

Day Seventeen

"Refusing to quit is the secret to unleashing rewards."

Some see returns in an instant. For others, it can take a lifetime. It took Craigen Armstrong three years in the pre-trial phase, twelve years on death row, and four more years back in the LA County Jail on an appeal, waiting to be retried. A total of twenty years incarcerated, and he refuses to stop his fight until he sees his reward.

DAY EIGHTEEN

"Change only happens when you want it."

Nobody will do it for you. People can hope for you, and doctors may suggest that you do. Family may urge you to. You may even have slight beliefs and convictions to change something, but until you really want it is when you will begin stepping toward your transformation.

DAY NINETEEN

"You will be greater than the mountain you are climbing."

A "G.O.A.T." of musical composition, Wolfgang Mozart was told by Emperor Ferdinand that his opera, *The Marriage of Figaro* was "far too noisy" and "contained far too many notes." Such grand remarks from a grand person (Mozart's mountain). Wolfgang Mozart not only made history, but sits on the tongues of the greatest composers to date– many years after his time.

DAY TWENTY

"Every move you make is an investment."

This philosophy will urge you to make every moment count. Life is the greatest opportunity humankind will know. So, will you take advantage of it? Or will you watch as your force to move withers away?

DAY TWENTY-ONE

"To envision yourself overcoming, is the first step to overcoming."

Create the picture in your mind. Color all the details. Feel the perspective. Taste your desired fantasy. Is it believable? To others, it may be unrealistic, but that doesn't matter! The real question is: do you hunger for this visual?

DAY TWENTY-TWO

"Hard work is encouragement to work hard."

The lazy, spoiled, slouch of a person will make intricacy discouraging. Yet, if you're up for the challenge, dedication, persistence and enthusiasm will create wonders and an abundance of rewards. The results will permit you to be proud.

Take the Shri Swaminarayan, a temple in Neasden, London, England. It's made of 2,565 tons of Bulgarian limestone, and 1,814 tons of Italian marble, which was first shipped to India to be carved by a team of 1,526 sculptors. This much hard labor truly is work to take pride in. If you have seen this temple, you will not deny this place as splendor and inspiration.

DAY TWENTY-THREE

"It's your choice to make the bitter things in life sweet."

Storms will come and go, physically, mentally, and emotionally; some not so harsh and many full of disaster. Will you be infected, or will you grab your coat, slip on some boots, and push open your umbrella? You really have the power to choose!

Day Twenty-Four

"You can find greatness in every weakness."

Statistics show that twenty percent of all fatal accidents occur in automobiles. This has caused all auto-businesses to up their safety measures and, therefore, bring in more sales, along with greater prices. They've taken full advantage of flaws, producing greater goods, while getting rich. Find the opportunities in your weaknesses. They may be the door you've been searching for.

Day Twenty-Five

"The wall was built. It can be broken down."

It may be big, tall, tough, painful, and scary. Plus, all the negative type of feelings it's founded on. But, trust me, that wall looks at the sledge hammer, wrecking ball, and most of all your attitude with that same kind of paradigm; and those tools are all in your reach.

DAY TWENTY-SIX

"Overtime sets apart the greater from the great."

The truth is: Overtime is the choice of the hungry individual.
How bad do you want it? When you're ready to eat, you won't just
think about it. You'll find yourself moving swiftly. Distinguishing
yourself from even those who float at the top.

DAY TWENTY-SEVEN

"What you put in the toilet is not all that's in you! Greatness awaits!"

The power to build and destroy. To give life or take it. So godlike! This is nothing compared to what you're capable of accomplishing. Be humble, but don't fool yourself out of the awesome design you were created to develop and perform in.

DAY TWENTY-EIGHT

"Ask more of yourself and you'll give."

The great teacher, Jesus of Nazareth, taught: "Ask and you shall receive." He wasn't lying! You yourself are the most willing to your direction. Just remember not to sell yourself short. You will forever deserve more of yourself. When you really want it, you'll really get it. Whenever, wherever that is. Go ahead, give it a spin.

DAY TWENTY-NINE

"You are the treasure, but you must not wait to be found."

Not many people search for potential. You must then see it for yourself. One's greatest discovery is in self. Then, your "might" shall show. Then, life will matter. You'll see if you haven't already. Watch!

DAY THIRTY

"To remain set back is not an option."

It happened. Now move on. Next is the path forward. When
you die, that's when you can settle; don't waste this opportunity
called living. Destroy that option. Rid that idea from your mind
FOREVER!

DAY THIRTY-ONE

"The bigger the mountain, the greater the view."

It is said the most beautiful sights take time to reach. The heights that must be climbed. The difficulties that must be conquered on the paths taken. Yet, the visual which stands waiting is very rewarding. Worth far more than the struggle's cost.

ABOUT THE AUTHOR

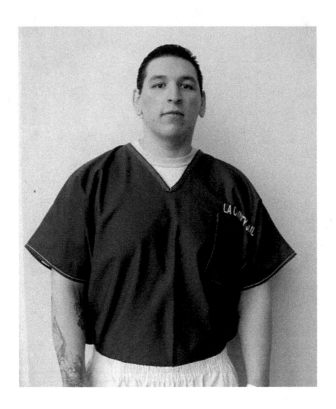

Adrian Berumen was incarcerated at the age of seventeen years old, in 2013 of April. Currently, he resides in the Los Angeles County Jail, awaiting trial. He is devoted to have a positive impact any chance given. He serves as a certified Mental Health Assistant, where he mentors and holds groups on life skills, purpose, and many more educational and inspirational subjects. Adrian is the co-author of "The Solution: Mental Health Assistant" – Available at store.bookbaby.com

CPSIA information can be obtained
at www.ICGtesting.com
Printed in the USA
BVHW040344011021
617866BV00015B/1128